Thomas Hardy in Wimborne
1881 - 1883

Brenda Flint

GH00707876

Power Publications, Ferndown in association with
The Priest's House Museum Trust
Wimborne Minster
1995

~ACKNOWLEDGEMENTS~

I am indebted to Stephen Price for his help and encouragement in preparing this material, and to Barbara Willis for her expertise in finding suitable illustrations. The staff at the Dorset County Library and Dorset County Museum are also thanked for their unfailing courteous assistance.

John Pentney of The Thomas Hardy Society and former Hardy editor, was kind enough to read the original manuscript and offer valuable criticism and advice. Any subsequent errors and omissions are, of course, entirely my own.

Illustrations

Front cover and Figure 1: Photograph of Thomas Hardy, circa 1880. by courtesy of The Dorset Natural History and Archaelogical Society, Dorset County Museum, Dorchester, Dorset.

Figures nos: 2, 4, 5, 6, 7, 8, 10, 13, 15, 17, 19, 21 by courtesy of The Priest's House Museum Trust.

Fig. no: 9 - Lanherne, by courtesy of Halifax Property Services.

Fig. nos. 12, 14, 18 by courtesy of The Dorset Natural History and Archaeological Society, Dorset County Museum.

Fig no: 20, Charborough Tower, by courtesy of Derek Willis.

Fig no: 23, frontispiece from the Wessex Edition of *Two on a Tower* by courtesy of HarperCollins

The remainder of the illustrations are from the author's collection.

Layout: Richard Broadway, East Dorset District Council.

~CONTENTS~

Fig. 1. Thomas Hardy, c.1880

~THOMAS AND EMMA~

When the Hardys arrived in Wimborne they had been married for nearly seven years and they were both over forty years old. Their idyllic sojourn in Sturminster Newton, 'our happiest time', was at an end. A cryptic entry appears in Hardy's diary of the period: 'The sudden disappointment of a hope leaves a scar which the ultimate fulfilment of that hope never entirely removes.' A note written in August 1877 gives a hint of their desire: 'We hear that Jane, our late servant is soon to have a baby. Yet never a sign of one is there for us.' The first flush of expectation and happiness had faded and they both felt it was time to make a change.

Although a Dorset man by birth, Hardy had been convinced that a move to London was essential to promote his writing career. He looked forward to achieving a wider social experience and opportunity within the literary circles and mental stimuli of the metropolis. They subsequently moved to Upper Tooting, but the reality of their life there turned out rather differently. As Hardy the novelist enjoyed increasing success with the publication of Far from the Madding Crowd, 1874, and The Return of the Native, 1878, (The Hand of Ethelberta was less successful) Hardy the man was experiencing worrying lassitude and depression. He fell prone to strange fancies. Waking in the early hours of the morning, London seemed to him to be a 'monster whose body had four million heads and eight million eyes.' A scathing review of The Return of the Native devastated him, particularly wounding was the criticism of his style and his use of dialect. Perversely, his latest novel, The Trumpet Major attracted very good reviews when serialized but in book form sales were poor. Finally, in 1880, Hardy became seriously ill suffering from inflammation of the bladder and internal bleeding. Emma nursed Hardy throughout the bitterly cold winter of 1880-81. He lay in bed with his legs raised, painfully dictating to her chapter after chapter of deteriorating prose. The first episode of A Laodicean commissioned by Harper's magazine, had already been printed so he had to carry on.

> 'January 1881. My third month in bed. Driving snow, fine and so fast that individual flakes cannot be seen... It creeps into the house, the window plants being covered as if out-of-doors. Our passage downstairs is sole-deep, Em says, and feet leave tracks on it.'

The Hardys' lease had expired on the preceding Lady Day, while Thomas was too ill to move. 'There is mercy in troubles coming in battalions – they neutralize each other' he comments wryly in his diary. It was May before he took his first walk outside alone. The problem of finding somewhere to live was acute and he pined for Dorset.

Fig. 2. The interior of Wimborne Minster (1839)

~THE TOWN OF WIMBORNE~

Hardy had visited the town previously on a house-hunting expedition, and would have passed through on the train many times. The circumstances were sufficiently romantic to warrant a mention in The Life...

'and thence to Wimborne, where on arrival he entered the Minster at ten at night, having seen a light within, and sat in a stall listening to the organist practising, while the rays from the musician's solitary candle streamed across the arcades.'

Hardy also knew something of the district through supervising the restoration of Hinton Martell Church. A plaque in the church porch records that 'THOMAS HARDY - Dorset author and architect - helped in the design and supervision of the re-building of this church in 1870.'

Fig. 3. Plaque of Hardy Restoration in Hinton Martell Church.
Fig. 4. Hinton Martell Church.

What kind of town welcomed the Hardys in 1881? A town of oil lamps and gas-light, where water was drawn from wells, where the hospital had yet to be built. It was a growing town and The Avenue, where the couple rented LANHERNE, was one of the newer districts. An important feature, as Hardy needed to visit London fairly frequently, was the railway. The rail network underpinned Wimborne's prosperity and the spreading town crept outwards to meet it. The parish of New Borough and Leigh had been formed in 1876, five years before the Hardys' arrival.

Fig. 5. St John's Church, Wimborne.

The new church, dedicated to St. John the Evangelist, was designed by architect Walter Fletcher, who was to become one of Hardy's firmest friends. But there were signs that the town was fast outgrowing its infrastructure. On 25 May 1882 a Government Enquiry, held at Wimborne, was reported in *The Poole and Dorset Herald*. It concerned the application of the sanitary authority... 'to extend the special drainage district so as to include several large houses and other property in the vicinity of Upper Avenue-road and Leigh-road... Mr. W. Druitt said he would like to see more ground taken in by the extension... The Cemetery, in particular, required draining, as the water running from it after heavy rains contaminated the wells in the lower parts of the district, especially as most of the wells were merely superficial ones, there being only about three deep wells in the whole of the town'.

Fig. 6. Lock's barber's shop, Cheapside, Wimborne.

Thomas used to visit Lock's in the High Street for a shave and a haircut, and, according to the barber's son who gave an interview to the *Wimborne District News* in 1951, George Macdonald Lock was immortalised as the barber in *The Woodlanders*.

Fig. 7. The barber's chair used by Thomas Hardy at Lock's.

Hé is also credited with telling Hardy the story of the wife who was sold in the New Inn (now The Albion) said to be a true incident, which provides the dramatic opening to *The Mayor of Casterbridge*. It must be said, however, that there are several such tales recorded in early nineteenth century Wessex and the Wimborne claim to be the original source cannot be proved.

In those days the young apprentices worked from eight in the morning until the Minster curfew rang at eight in the evening. There was a wide variety of shops in the town. Hardy had a choice of six booksellers, printers and stationers to gratify his literary needs. Emma found at least six butchers and several grocers, dressmakers and shoe sellers. Not all the older trades had disappeared, there were two millers and seven blacksmiths. The cattle market was held once a week and gypsies camped by the side of Leigh Road. Murray's Handbook for 1882 describes Wimborne like this:-

'Wimborne Stat. (The town lies 3/4m. N.W. Omnibuses meet every train.) (Inns: Crown; King's Head; Railway Hotel. Pop.5938)... It is a clean, neat, and pleasant town. The Somerset and Dorset Rly. branches off here by Blandford to Temple Combe and Glastonbury, and joins the Great Western at Highbridge.'

Fig. 8. Wimborne railway station, since demolished.

The Hardys arrived in the heyday of the railway when the town was the most important junction and depot in the county. Several years later its importance was diminished by a loop line routing Somerset and Dorset line trains from Bath direct to Poole without the need to pass through Wimborne.

There was a colony of railway workers at the lower end of Avenue-road, close to the station. Here lived the porters, a signalman, engine drivers, railway firemen, railway clerks, a telegraph clerk, the ticket collector and the Station Master, C. William Edwards, who hailed from Lyme Regis. Coal merchants and coal agents found it convenient to live near the station too.

At the other end of the Avenue, closer to St. John's Church, lived several retired gentlemen, a veterinary surgeon, the Wesleyan Minister and a retired grocer, John Low, with his wife Emily and their small daughter. The Low family had moved to Avenue-road from the High Street where their former shop premises are now occupied by the Priest's House Museum.

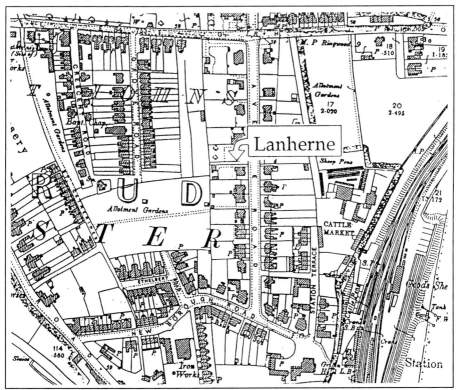

Fig. 9. From Ordnance Survey 1:2500 Map published 1901.

~THE HOUSE IN THE AVENUE~

Florence Hardy in *The Life* refers to 'a little house that would be suitable as a temporary measure until they found a better one or perhaps built one.' The house was built in 1872 and can be seen in Avenue Road today, with its blue and white plaque: ' Thomas Hardy lived here 1881 - 1883'.

Fig. 10. Lanherne, The Avenue, Wimborne.

A solid, well built house with brick walls under a slate roof, it has six rooms upstairs, and a sitting room, dining room, kitchen and conservatory downstairs. In Hardy's day the lavatory would have been in the garden - he had to wait until 1920 before he had a proper bathroom. Behind the house there was a mature garden and beyond the garden there were stables and a roomy coach house. As Hardy did not intend to use these himself, he offered them to a twenty-year old Scot, Frank (Francis I.) Douglas, who was lodging in Leigh Road, just round the corner, with Julian Vyse, aged 21, from Slough. According to the 1881 census, the two students were 'learning land agency' in Wimborne. Through Frank, Hardy met his elder brother Sir George Douglas, land-owner of Springwood Park, Kelso, and author of *A Love's Gamut and Other Poems*, 1880, and *Gleanings in Poetry and Verse*. Sir George had already written a rather fulsome sonnet 'to the author of *Far from the Madding Crowd*' and was to remain a life-long friend.

*Fig. 11. The plaque commemorating
Hardy's residence in Wimborne at Lanherne.*

Outside the house, The Avenue was newly planted with young lime trees. Years later, in 1918, a letter from Sir George brought back memories of the Wimborne years and prompted a few lines of Hardy's verse:

> They are great trees, no doubt, by now,
> That were so thin in bough -
> That row of limes -
> When we housed there; I'm loth to reckon when;
> The world has turned so many times,
> So many, since then! [1]

Fig. 12. The Avenue, Wimborne, c.1903

The couple moved in on June 25 1881 and on the first night they looked out from the conservatory and watched Tebbutt's Comet sail across the sky. Hardy found much to delight him there:

> 'Our garden has all sorts of old-fashioned flowers in full bloom: Canterbury Bells, blue and white, and Sweet Williams of every variety, strawberries and cherries that are ripe, currants and gooseberries that are almost ripe, peaches that are green, and apples that are decidedly immature.'

In July, Hardy hired a wagonette from the George Inn in the Cornmarket, and drove round the surrounding countryside with Emma and his sister Kate. The driver, William Young, took them past Kingston Lacy House, where he told a tale about young Walter Ralph Bankes and a certain old gentleman's young wife. They drove along the avenue of beeches, 'large in the hollows, small on the hills', Hardy noted, and visited Badbury Rings.

Later in the day, driving westwards, they passed Charborough Park, the property of Miss Drax '- a quiet little lady - keeps no company'. The gossiping driver told them it was 'heiress land', Miss Drax inheriting the property on her mother's death in 1853. Old Drax (her father) lived at Holnest where he spent his time rehearsing his own funeral. As the young Lieutenant John Sawbridge, with the help of a friendly parson, he had courted and won Jane Erle-Drax, he being very handsome and she 'not in her first bloom' and twelve years his senior. He adopted the surname and arms of Erle-Drax on their marriage in 1827. A similar relationship, that of an older woman and a younger socially inferior man, later became the romantic theme of *Two on A Tower*.

At the time, though, Hardy appears to have been more interested in the working life of the driver. Eight pages of the personal notebooks[2] are devoted to William Young's reminiscences. He jotted down notes about the stables in the old days, the head ostler who gave the orders, the 2d. and 3d. ostlers, the horse keeper and the one postillion to every four horses. He described the ceremonies of Assize week in Dorchester, with two carriages for the first judge, the second one for his books - a very heavy weight sometimes requiring 6 horses. The carriages stopped at the King's Arms in Puddletown where the judge donned his robes.

Fig. 13. The George Inn, Cornmarket, Wimborne.

Then at Yellowham Hill he was met by the sheriff and javelin men before proceeding to the judges lodging where the postboys were given a meal. The second judge arrived a few hours later with less pomp. William Young could remember driving along the Blandford road when it was so dark that he had to feel his way along the hedge with his whip. By the time Hardy talked to him, he was suffering from 'rheumatic gout' brought on by exposure to the elements, and his right leg was discoloured from the constant rub of the carriage pole against it. He complained that he could no longer get the beer he liked, home brewed, 12 bushels to the hogshead, and the colour of port wine. (A William Young aged 64, Post boy, Leigh Road, appears in the 1881 Wimborne Census.)

Hardy's spirits were improving daily. He began to jot down notes on the writing of fiction, possibly with a future article in mind. By August he felt well enough to undertake a tour of Scotland with Emma. After the holiday and home again in Wimborne, it was warm enough for Hardy to sit in the September sunshine to correct proofs of *A Laodicean* for issue in book form.

He would place his chair under the vine cladding the stable wall:

> '... which for want of training hangs in long arms over my head nearly to the ground. The sun shines through the great leaves, making a green light on the paper, the tendrils twisting in every direction, in gymnastic endeavours to find something to lay hold of.'

Fig. 14. Badbury Rings early this century

His creative impulse revived. The literary notebook of the period is full of quotations from the works of R.A. Proctor (1837-1888) who was a great popularizer of astronomy, the Patrick Moore of his day. The vastness and the mystery of the universe had always played on Hardy's imagination and, as he made very plain to his publishers, he had no intention of writing for ever about sheep farming, in spite of popular demand. What he now planned was a presentation of 'infinitesimal lives against the stupendous background of the stellar universe'.

When in October Hardy was asked to provide a serial for *The Atlantic Monthly*, his theme was ready made. The following month he applied to the Astronomer Royal for permission to visit Greenwich observatory but he met with a set-back; before his application could be considered he was obliged to state whether his visit was for astronomical and scientific reasons or not. Hardy, tongue in cheek, replied with a spoof scientific letter, written as though from the hero of his proposed novel.

He wished to know, he wrote, if it would be possible to adapt an old tower in the West of England for use in the telescopic study of the stars 'by a young man very ardent in that pursuit?' Permission to view the observatory duly arrived. In December he corresponded with William Cawthorne Unwin, the engineer, gleaning information about the technical aspects of telescopes and lens grinding.

Throughout the autumn of 1881 Hardy was working hard. Between proof correcting and researching his next novel he wrote two short stories.[3] He was convinced now that London had been a mistake, adversely affecting both his writing style and his health. But he was strong enough to risk a visit in December with Emma, to meet old friends and to finalize business arrangements with the publishers of *The Atlantic Monthly* magazine.

It was at about this time that Hardy renewed acquaintance with Sir Arthur Blomfield, the architect who employed him in the 1860's as an assistant. His first words to Hardy were: 'Do you remember how we found the man with two heads at St.Pancras?

The Minster green, Hardy noticed, was bare of tombstones and at a level considerably higher than the road, prompting memories of his personal experience of dealing with an inconvenient graveyard. Some fifteen years earlier, as Arthur Blomfield's assistant, he was involved in the re-burial of bodies which had to be removed to make way for the new Midland Railway cutting due to run through Old St.Pancras churchyard.

Blomfield had been shaken by the dubious methods of a contractor he had employed on a previous occasion. The ground where the bodies were re-buried, he was told, had proved on inspection to be suspiciously flat and undisturbed; worse - there were rumours of rattling sacks being delivered to the bone mills at dead of night. At Old St.Pancras there must be no scandal. The clerk-of-works was forbidden to leave the site. Hardy was detailed to make spot checks on the clerk and the labourers and Blomfield monitored them all.

Exhumation was carried out behind screens at night by the light of flarelamps and new coffins replaced the old to enable the bodies to be moved with dignity. Out of one crumbling box fell a skeleton with two skulls. The man with two heads. Sauntering around the Minster, Hardy's sardonic humour turned into verse. One of the stanzas read, in his manuscript:

> Where we are huddled none can trace,
> And if our names remain
> They paved some path or p.....g place
> Where we have never lain![4]

The poem was published much later and survived several editions in this form until an eagle-eyed editor substituted 'porch or' for 'pissing', the errata slip possibly attracting more attention to Hardy's earthier version.

Fig. 15. The Minster green before levelling

~THE SOCIAL SCENE~

The Hardys had expected to feel a little lonely in Wimborne where they had no close friends. They were agreeably surprised by being gently absorbed into Wimborne society which, if less grand than London, was less competitive.

Towards the end of their first year they were invited to a ball at Canford Manor by Lady Wimborne. Lord Wimborne confided his problems with dampness in the manor caused, he was sure, by the miller below penning water for grinding. When Hardy suggested that the mill might be removed, Lord Wimborne indignantly retorted that this would be impossible since the miller paid him £50 a year in rent. Hardy was glad, he had as much distaste for destroying a mill where they ground food for the body as for destroying a church where they ground food for the soul, he said.

Fig. 16. Canford Mill before 1894.

The visit to Canford Manor left Hardy with two vivid and lasting impressions. The shooting parties (whose large bags of game birds were avidly reported in the local press)[5] distressed him. His opinion was made clear in *Tess of the d'Urbervilles*:

'... these men... a bloodthirsty light in their eyes... were, in fact, quite civil persons save during certain weeks in autumn and winter, when, like the inhabitants of the Malay Peninsular, they ran amuck, and made it their purpose to destroy life - in this case harmless feathered creatures, brought into being by artificial means solely to gratify these propensities...'

However, impressed by the architecture and antiquity of parts of the Manor itself, Hardy used it as a model for Chene Manor, the family seat of *Barbara of the House of Grebe*. [6] In the story he describes the manor as 'an imposing edifice'...'One wing showed extreme antiquity, having huge chimneys, whose substructures projected from the external walls like towers; and a kitchen of vast dimensions, in which (it was said) breakfasts had been cooked for John of Gaunt.'

Fig. 17 and 18. Canford Manor and John of Gaunt's Kitchen

Newman and Pevsner in their survey of Dorset (1972) in *The Buildings of England* series, refer to Canford Manor (now Canford School) as 'A mighty C15 kitchen and a mighty C19 mansion'...'The so-called John of Gaunt's kitchen, lying N of the screen wall, is the medieval survivor'...'Also, rare survival, the original louvred chimneys'.

E arly in the new year they were invited to take part in Shakespeare readings organised by Dr.George Batterbury of West Borough. The young doctor (he was 31) called Hardy 'reticent'. Hardy complained that '...The host was omnivorous of parts - absorbing other people's besides his own, and was greedily vexed when I read a line of his part by mistake.' In any case, Hardy was busily observing, as novel writers do observe, the firelight shining as the day diminished, the young girl crouching on a foot stool, 'the wealthy Mrs. B. impassive and grand in her unintelligence, like a Carthaginian statue...'and the General [possibly Major General Maclean of Rowlands Hill] who read cautiously in perpetual fear of blurting out one of Shakespeare's improprieties. On the other hand, Tindal Atkinson's reading of Shylock was a dramatic *tour de force*.

In the spring the Hardys were out and about again, travelling to Liverpool to watch a dramatization of *Far from the Madding Crowd* - not to Hardy's liking and it made him no profit. In April he attended the funeral of Charles Darwin in London; as a young man he had greatly admired Darwin's *The Origin of Species*. Throughout the summer he worked in the garden whenever possible.

> 'August. This month blackbirds and thrushes creep about under fruit bushes and in other shady places in gardens rather like four-legged animals than birds... I notice that a blackbird has eaten nearly a whole pear lying in the garden-path in the course of the day.'

On September 9th, Dr. and Mrs. Brine came to tea. John Brine and his wife Ann both came from Somerset. They lived in Rowlands Hill in rather grander style than Dr. Batterbury. Their establishment included a cook, house-keeper, general servant and a groom. Ann Brine came from Wincanton, and her husband told Hardy that Jack White's gibbett close by the town was standing as late as 1835 - 'i.e. the oak-post with the iron arm sticking out and a portion of the cage in which the body had formerly hung...' Next door to the Brines lived Hardy's wealthiest and most influential friend. Henry Tindal Atkinson, a widower of 75, and his unmarried daughter Louisa, entertained the Hardys at Uplands to musical evenings. His married daughter Emma and her husband Ambrose Stokes, a retired merchant, visited now and then. Tindal Atkinson was a county court judge and one of the last to hold the ancient title of Serjeant-at-Law, and if the epitaph on his gravestone in Wimborne cemetery is true of the man, then his outlook on life was, unlike Hardy's, heroically optimistic:

One who never turned his back but marched
breast forward
Never doubted clouds would break,
Never dream'd tho' right were worsted, wrong
would triumph,
Held we fall to rise, are baffled to fight better,
sleep to wake.

But he proved to be a true friend, offering helpful advice when Hardy was concerned about possible plagiarism of *Far from the Madding Crowd*. A play by Pinero, *The Squire*, about a young woman farmer, resembled his novel and his own dramatization. The judge told him about a case 'on all fours with yours' but it transpired that the similarities were not close enough to warrant serving a writ. It was particularly galling for Hardy to learn that *The Squire* was more successful than his own play. He put it down to the part of the mad parson written into the play for John Hare, which went down well with audiences, and it may well be that this influenced his much criticised treatment of the clergy in *Two on a Tower*.

Walter Fletcher, architect and county surveyor, was a most congenial companion. He lived with his wife Augusta and three very young children in the Chantry, Grammar School Lane, opposite the Minster. Walter was an interesting man with a fund of local stories, and he shared Hardy's fondness for walking. On February 28 1883, the two men walked to Corfe Mullen and on the way Fletcher described the curious auction of turnpike tolls held at a local inn. The auctioneer and the trustees sat at one end of the room and at the other end there was 'a crowd of strange beings, looking as not worth sixpence among them'. The bidders would step outside frequently for private consultation and on returning only one or two of them would bid. Obviously there was a ring at work and it is not surprising to learn that some promoters of turnpike trusts lost money. The coming of the railway was the last nail in the coffin. When the Puddletown and Wimborne Trust ceased in 1878, it was estimated that Erle-Drax of Charborough Park had lost £48,000[7].

On the road to Corfe Mullen the two friends were invited into an old house, formerly an inn, a smugglers' haunt. The owner showed them into the stable and pointed out the farthest stall, where a man had been killed after a quarrel. If a horse is left in the stall on certain nights, he told them, at about two in the morning (the time at which the smuggler was killed) it cries like a child and becomes lathered with sweat. In the trunk of the dead chestnut tree outside they found the hooks where smugglers had hitched their horses in the past.

It is a moot point whether Hardy actively sought stories about death in its strangest aspects or whether they came his way fortuitously. A few weeks later his servant Ann was regaling him with the tale of the carpenter and the coffin (verified, noted Hardy.) The carpenter who made a coffin for a certain Mr.W. made it too short. A bystander jeered at the small man - 'Anybody would think you'd made it for yourself, John!' The carpenter said 'Ah - they would!' and dropped down dead. Hardy enjoyed chatting with the servants. Notes left by Montague Harvey (in The Priest's House Museum) tell of a cook his mother's family employed at Oakley after she had left the Hardy household. This cook had a broad Dorset accent and told the Fenners that Thomas spent some time most days in the kitchen, laughing with the domestic staff and encouraging them to talk to him. Then he would disappear into his study, the room behind the conservatory, for the rest of the day. She regarded Emma as a somewhat eccentric lady, because she always wore her hair in pigtails and she rode a tricycle.

Fig. 19. The Chantry, Wimborne (since destroyed).

Hardy's preoccupation with death, or death in life, surfaced again at an Ambulance Society lecture he attended with Emma, when he noticed a skeleton hung upside down inside the window. 'We face it as we sit. Outside the band is playing and the children are dancing. I can see their little figures through the window past the skeleton dangling in front.'

The close of their second year in Wimborne brought wintry weather. Hardy mentions hearing about an open cart driving through freezing rain when the passengers became literally packed with ice. 'Getting one of the men into the house was like bringing in a chandelier of lustres'.

~TWO ON A TOWER~

In vision I roamed the flashing Firmanent,
So fierce in blazon that the Night waxed wan.[8]

The tragi-comedy romance *Two on a Tower* was the culmination of Hardy's fascination with the cosmos. Fate, the Immanent Will, or the magic hand of chance, conspired to provide him with the inspiration, the plot and the location all within a few weeks of his arrival in Wimborne. By coincidence, the final consultation after his serious illness in London was with Sir Henry Thompson, a keen amateur astronomer with plans to build a private observatory. By coincidence, on his first night in Wimborne he witnessed the passing of Tebbutt's comet. By coincidence, a month later, he drove past Charborough Park with its hilltop tower, when the garrulous driver gossiped about the well-to-do lady who married a handsome young man many years her junior.

Murray's Handbook of 1882 tells us that Charborough tower was erected by Major Drax in 1790 and rebuilt in 1839 after being struck by lightning. He describes it as a 'conspicuous object for miles around'. Sir Frederick Treves, less kindly, says it looks like a factory chimney, adding: 'It has been described as an example of "the most distinctive and aggressive Strawberry Hill Gothic" '. Hardy's words - '.... the pillar rose into the sky a bright and cheerful thing, unimpeded, clean and flushed with sunlight', are more in keeping with the classical column of the Tuscan order he chose to represent his imaginative romantic setting.

Hardy moulds his Wessex to suit his literary needs. He had as much compunction about relocating features of Dorset landscape as he had in shifting the skeletons of Old St. Pancras Churchyard. In his preface of July 1895, the author states: 'The scene of the action was suggested by two spots in the part of the county specified, each of which has a column standing upon it...' One spot was the tower in Charborough Park, named 'Rings-Hill Speer' in the novel, the 'speer' deriving from the second spot, the obelisk in the wood on the top of Weatherbury castle, near Puddletown. Welland House, although based on Charborough House, is placed arbitrarily on the right hand side of the road from Warborne (Wimborne).

At that time he had not set foot in the house and descriptions of the interior are purely imaginary. In fact his first sight of the interior was in October 1927 when he and his wife lunched at Charborough House. The railway plays an important part in the novel, though railway buffs would find it difficult to reconcile nineteenth century timetables with the plot. The junction appears to have been imported imaginatively purely to assist the story, since the train from Bath to Wimborne was a through train and neither was there need to change trains from Salisbury to Wimborne. Hardy found most of his information about Charborough in one of his favourite sources Hutchins's *History and Antiquities of the County of Dorset*.

Fig. 20. Charborough Tower

It would be difficult to better Hardy's own précis of the plot - 'Being the story of the unforeseen relations into which a lady and a youth many years her junior were drawn by studying the stars together; of her desperate situation through generosity to him, and of the reckless *coup d'audace* by which she effected her deliverance.'

Fig. 21. The Grammar School (now converted into private houses).

The town of Warborne is peripheral to the story. Warborne Grammar School (The Queen Elizabeth Grammar School) receives a highly coloured commendation when Lady Constantine asks Amos Fry (known as Haymoss) where Swithin St.Cleeve was educated.

> 'At Warborne, - a place where they draw up young gam'sters' brains like rhubarb under a ninepenny pan, my lady... They hit so much learning into en that a could talk like the day of Pentecost, which is a wonderful thing for a simple boy, and his mother only the plainest ciphering woman...'

St.Cleeve's father, the curate, had made a 'terrible bruckle hit' by marrying beneath his social station.

To preserve the secret of their love affair, Lady Constantine and Swithin walked from Warborne Station towards Welland separately, 'till they had reached a shadowy bend in the old turnpike road, beyond the irradiation of Warborne lamplight' (probably Pye Corner in those days). The lovers were glad of the darkness which concealed their association but the residents of Wimborne had reason to complain of inadequate street lighting.

This is borne out by a report in *The Poole and Bournemouth Herald,* November 17 1881, of a serious accident in which a bricklayer was knocked down by a horse and trap on his way home from work... 'No blame attached to the driver, but it is to be hoped that the want of lamps along the Leigh-road will soon be taken into consideration by the authority responsible for the lighting of the town'.

Imagery of light and the night-time sky is sustained throughout the novel. A scene in the church at Welland is reminiscent of Hardy's first visit to the Minster. Lady Constantine sat in the church at dusk 'where the feeble glimmer from the candle of the organist spread a glow-worm radiance around'. During the early summer while Swithin is lying ill in bed, Lady Constantine (Viviette) watched Tebbutt's comet, as Hardy had watched it, 'that visitant of singular shape and habits which had appeared in the sky from no one knew whence, trailing its luminous streamer...' Towards the end of the book. when Swithin returns to a 'worn and faded' Viviette, '... the masses of hair that were once darkness visible had become touched here and there by a faint grey haze, like the Via Lactea in a midnight sky'.

Gittings tells us that in the summer of 1881, soon after the Hardys came to Wimborne, Francis Jeune, brother-in-law of Canon Gifford, Emma's uncle, married the widow of Col. the Hon. John Constantine Stanley, giving Emma a tentative entrée into high society. From Mrs. Jeune's first husband Hardy is said to have taken his second name and the man's unpleasant personality for the fictional character Sir Blount Constantine. Another possibility is that through his interest in local history, Hardy had come across Constantine of Merley, a 'rotten commoner' who was sent to London in custody with his brother-in-law John Hanham in 1644. There is also a monument to Harry Constantine, 1712, and others of his family in the north nave aisle of Wimborne Minster, and there were Blounts in Rowlands Hill living close to Hardy's friends.

More interestingly, Gittings makes a connection between the Tichborne case and the sub-plot concerning the mysterious disappearance, reported death, false reappearance and death of Sir Blount Constantine. As a junior, the lawyer Francis Jeune appeared for Orton who was the imposter claiming the Tichborne inheritance. This story would have appealed to Hardy.

Fig. 22. Blandford Lodge, Charborough Park.

Two on a Tower was the last Wessex novel to have an almost happy ending. Swithin promises to look after his natural son after Viviette's death and there is Tabitha Lark waiting in the wings 'the single bright spot of colour and amination within the wide horizon.' The novel was written at a steady rate throughout 1882, apart from a break when the Hardys made a tour of the west country. There was pressure, as usual, in keeping up monthly instalments for publication simultaneously in America and England. The novel was published in book form in October 1882; Hardy himself admitting that it had not had his full creative attention.

~THE REVIEWS~

The critics were not kind. The editor of *The Atlantic Monthly* is reputed to have complained that instead of the promised family story he had been sent a story in the family way. Viviette's deception of the Bishop of Melchester was viewed generally as 'extremely repulsive'. Only Charles Kegan Paul, the reviewer and publisher, who formerly spent twelve years as the Vicar of Sturminster Marshall, a few miles from Wimborne, thought it was 'a marvellously comic touch' that the victim was a bishop. Hardy was naively astounded that the *coup d'audace* enraged so many people. But even in the freewheeling late twentieth century, the notion of a well born lady deceiving a bishop by accepting his proposal of marriage while carrying another man's child would be unacceptable, even if he were a pompous ass. Hardy, of course, thought he had put matters right with his somewhat perfunctory ending: 'Viviette was dead. The Bishop was avenged'.

Today the novel is considered to be one of Hardy's minor works, but nevertheless one in which he was honing his technique and refining his artistic vision. The grand theme of man measured against the universe failed because his characters were not strong enough and their love affair was half-hearted. Viviette was not pitiable like Tess, nor was Swithin a strong constant lover like Gabriel Oak, in *Far from the Madding Crowd* or Giles Winterborne in *The Woodlanders*. Hardy's references to the ancient past - '...old Roman camp...', '...palaeolithic dead men feeding the roots of the forest round it' (the tower) - did not connect properly with the story. As Hornback points out: 'The metaphor of history... can only support a character it cannot make one'. And while some critics admired the astronomical details in the book, it must be said that Hardy's research showed and failed to merge naturally into the story.

One last coincidence concerns *Two on a Tower*. In March 1895, long after the Hardys had left Wimborne, Macbeth Raeburn was visiting places in Wessex to make sketches for etchings commissioned by the publishers of the Wessex novels. At Charborough Park he met with a firm refusal to his request to sketch the house; he was threatened with the bailiff. However, he hid behind a tree and began to draw secretly when suddenly the bailiff came running up and ordered him out of the park.

Raeburn was just leaving when he turned and said 'surely you come from my country?' They discovered not only that they were both Scots but that they had grown up in the same village. The bailiff relented and told him to draw wherever he wanted 'but don't let her see you from the winders'. Raeburn's sketch was used as the frontispiece for the Wessex edition of the novel.

Fig. 23. Macbeth Raeburn's sketch of Charborough Park

Thomas and Emma were able to escape the controversy aroused by his novel by visiting Paris, where they spent a happy few weeks browsing round art galleries, shopping for food and housekeeping like native Parisians in the apartment they rented near the Left Bank.

~THE LAST SIX MONTHS~

In December 1882, Hardy, as he records in *The Life*, met an old country woman who told him a story about a young girl who had been seduced and deserted by her lover. The girl decided to keep the child and bring him up by herself. Hardy was very impressed with this example of early feminism. The idea of a woman's independence, the refusal to surrender her future to her seducer, threads through several of his later works and poems, most famously in *Tess of the d'Urbervilles*. The same month saw the publication of the short story 'A Tradition of Eighteen Hundred and Four' written the previous summer.

Early in 1883 two more short stories were published: *'The Three Strangers'* rather a grim dramatic story, and *'The Romantic Adventures of a Milkmaid'*, a Cinderella tale of an innocent heroine, a wicked baron, a ball, a carriage, and a happy ending. Much later, in 1927, Hardy wrote to F. Macmillan expressing regret over this conventional conclusion with the convenient death of the baron.

Although he was working well in Wimborne, Hardy was not entirely satisfied with life and Emma craved the kind of high society she thought was her due. Both complained about the low-lying town and the nearness of the river which they imagined had a detrimental effect on their health. But during his stay in Wimborne Hardy began to develop the interest in history and social concerns that were to pervade his later work. In 1882 he joined the Dorset Natural History And Antiquarian Field Club which had its headquarters in Dorchester. He also concerned himself with cruelty to animals, ably abetted by Emma who was not afraid to complain loudly and volubly on the spot if she saw an animal being abused.

Before leaving Wimborne Hardy began writing *'The Dorsetshire Labourer'*, a serious essay for Longman's magazine. In this work Hardy demolished the myth of the stereotyped farm labourer Hodge, '… a degraded being of uncouth manner and aspect, stolid understanding, and snail-like movement.' Instead, he celebrates the diversity of character, skills and opinions found in country workfolk. He explains the subtle differences in social standing, particularly between the regular labourers and those 'unattached' who while out of sight of patronage are also 'out of mind when misfortune arises'. The greatest fear is that of losing the roof over their heads.

Descriptions of the annual hiring fair at Candlemas and the subsequent 'musical chairs' movement of farm workers on Lady Day, are well known from his novels. But in the article Hardy discusses the advantages of change, which enables the labourers to widen their experience, becoming 'shrewder and sharper men of the world'. On the other hand, he deplores the loss of contact with their familiar environment and the 'long local participancy which is one of the pleasures of age.' We are reminded that over a hundred years ago the settled country community was already in the past and villages were becoming denuded of their small traders and artisans, while cottages not needed for farm workers were demolished wholesale impelling a population drift to urban centres. Hardy likens the process to that of 'the tendency of water to flow uphill when forced.'

He was a great admirer of Joseph Arch* and went to one of his meetings, where he was impressed by the speaker's moderate tone - rather the 'social evolutionist' than the 'anarchic irreconcilable' , he thought. The movement, which culminated in the formation of a National Agricultural Labourer's Union in May 1872, was started by Joseph Arch, a hedger and ditcher who developed his oratory skill as a Methodist lay preacher and later became a liberal M.P. Hardy credits him with bringing about an average rise of three shillings a week in Dorset labourers' wages (in those times amounting to an increase of between 30% and 40%). However, the greatest success of Arch's union came about in 1884, the year after Hardy left Wimborne, when its pressure played a large part in extending Parliamentary franchise so that many farm labourers attained the vote. Joseph Arch was highly critical of 'tied' cottages and at the end of his article Hardy equates the question of the Dorset cottager with the problems raised by all the homeless and landless poor and 'the vast topic of the Rights of Man'. It is our loss that he considered this theme to be '... beyond the scope of a merely descriptive article.'

* ARCH, Joseph (1826 - 1919), politician; itinerant agricultural labourer, 1835 - 72; instrumental in forming Warwickshire Agricultural Labourer's Union 1872; organising secretary (afterwards president) of newly founded National Agricultural Labourers' Union, 1872; Liberal MP, North-west Norfolk 1885-6, 1892-1902.

~THOMAS & EMMA~
AFTER WIMBORNE

SINE PROLE
Forth from ages thick in mystery,
Through the morn and noon of history,
To the moment where I stand
Has my line wound; I the last one -
Outcome of each spectral past one
Of that file, so many-manned![9]

(Sine Prole - without offspring).

In June 1883 the Hardys moved from Wimborne to Dorchester where the family face was all about them. 'The hands of the generations' would not be continuing for them, fate had decreed otherwise. Hardy poured his creative powers into his work, tragedy deepening in each novel until his bitterness was spent in *Jude The Obscure*, the one work Emma could neither condone nor forgive.

Was their marriage the outright disaster some biographers describe? Sir George Douglas, who knew the Hardys well when they lived in Wimborne and kept in close touch with them for many years afterwards, thought otherwise. To his mind, Emma and Thomas were as well assorted as many of the happily married couples that one comes across in life, 'each had sacrificed something to the other'. Sir George regarded the Wimborne interlude as a happy period in Hardy's life and the two years the novelist spent in the town did much to restore his health and good spirits, free from family friction and the pressures that were to come 'in battalions' when his fame was at its height.

~NOTES~

1. 'They are Great Trees'. First published in *The Life. Complete Poems No.943.*

2. *The Personal Notebooks of Thomas Hardy. Memoranda 1.* edited by R.H.Taylor, 1978.

3. 'Benighted Travellers' (later re-titled 'The Honourable Laura' and 'What the Shepherd Saw').

4. 'The Levelled Churchyard' *Complete Poems No. 127.*

5. *The Poole & Dorset Herald*, 8th December 1881.

6. From *A Group of Noble Dames*, 1891.

7. Somerset & Dorset Notes and Queries, 17 (1923), 52.

8. 'In Vision I Roamed'. *Complete Poems No. 690.*

9. 'Sine Prole'. *Complete Poems No. 690.*

The Priest's House Museum Trust, a registered charity, operates East Dorset's Museum Service from the historic Priest's House Museum in the centre of Wimborne Minster. Its aims are to research, collect, conserve and make available, through exhibition and publication, objects and associated evidence depicting the history of East Dorset.

~SELECT BIBLIOGRAPHY~

Gittings, R.   *The Older Hardy*, 1978, paperback edition 1980.

Hardy, T.   *Two on a Tower*, 1882. New Wessex edition, 1975.

Hardy, T.   *The Complete Poems*. edited by J. Gibson, 1976

Hardy, T.   *Collected Short Stories*, edited by R.H. Taylor, 1978.

Hardy, T.   *The Life and Work of Thomas Hardy*, edited by M.
                  Millgate, 1982, 1987 edition (an edition on new princi-
                  pals of the materials previously drawn upon for *The Early
                  Life of Thomas Hardy* 1840 -1891 and *The Later Years of
                  Thomas Hardy 1892 - 1928*, published over the name of
                  Florence Emily Hardy).

Hornback, B.G.   *The Metaphor of Chance, Vision and Technique in the
                  Works of Thomas Hardy*, Ohio, 1971.

Hutchins, J.   *The History and Antiquities of the County of Dorset*. 1st.
                  edition Vols. 1 and 2, 1774; 3rd. edition, 4 Vols. 1861-70

James, J.   *Wimborne Minster - The History of a Country Town.*
                  Wimborne, 1982.

Millgate, M.   *Oxford Lives. Thomas Hardy*. 1982, 1987 edition.

Murry, J.   *Handbook for Travellers in Wiltshire, Dorsetshire, and
                  Somersetshire*. edited by E.V. 1882.

Pentney, J.C.   *The Country of 'Two on a Tower'*. The Thomas Hardy
                  Society. Dorchester, 1982.

Popham, D.   *The Book of Wimborne*. Buckingham, 1983.

Treves, Sir F.   *Highways and Byways of Dorsetshire*, 1905.

Wimborne History Workshop. *Wimborne in the Nineteenth Century*, edited
by J. James. W.E.A., Southampton, 1978.

The Poole and Dorset Herald and *Poole and Bournemouth Herald* 1881-
1883, files in Dorset County Library, Dorchester.

Thomas Hardy Year Book, No. 14, 1986.

Unpublished material in the Priest's House Museum library:

The Hardy File.
Transcript of the 1881 census for Wimborne.